Removing Barriers to State Occupational Licenses To Enhance Entrepreneurial Job Growth:

Out of Prison & Out of Work

Chris Edwards

Author of 90 Days to a Glass Half Full

Lifestyle & 2 Hours Unplugged: Unplug & Reconnect

Other Books by San Francisco Bay Area Author Chris Edwards

- 90 Days to a Glass Half Full Lifestyle
- 2 Hours Unplugged: Unplug & Reconnect
- Coach Robert Louis Sepulveda The Early Days
- Coach Robert Louis Sepulveda The Golden Years
- Get Fuc-ing Right, Get Real Harsh Affirmations for Tough Times

To learn more or to follow the author visit

- https://authorchrisedwards.com/
- https://www.amazon.com/Chris-Edwards/e/B07RPCCCWC/ref=ntt_dp_epwbk_0
- https://2ndlifemedia.com/

Copyright © 2019 Chris Edwards (Martin Christopher Edwards) 2nd Life Media

All rights reserved. This book may not be reproduced in any form, in whole or in part (beyond the copying permitted by the US Copyright Law, Section 107, "fair use" in teaching or research, Section 108, certain library copying, or in published media by reviews in limited excerpts), without written permission of author.

Disclaimer

This book is for educational, entertainment and policy discussion purposes only. The views or opinions expressed, and life experience observations are of the author alone backed by sourced data where applicable. The reader is responsible for his or her own mindset, actions, and beliefs. Adherence to all applicable laws and regulations, including international, federal, state, and local governing professional licensing, personal conduct, business or personal practices, advertising and all other aspects of doing business or conducting oneself lawfully is the sole responsibility of the purchaser or the reader. Neither the author nor the publisher nor any other person nor affiliated or nonaffiliated business nor individual assumes any liability or responsibility whatsoever on behalf of the purchaser or reader of these materials. The purchaser or reader assumes full personal responsibility for their own actions and agrees to hold all others harmless. This book serves as a policy recommendation brief.

Copyright © 2019 Chris Edwards (Martin C Edwards) 2nd Life Media

Barriers to Employment

Forward by the Author

    This work is a collaborative work for the benefit of criminal justice reform. As an individual that was professionally employed and made a serious mistake, paid my time and am now a contributor of society I know firsthand of the barriers to successful re-entry.

    I was fortunate as I had a robust support system with loyal friends and family that ensured my success post incarceration for tax fraud. Through that experience I grew but was also educated to the issues of disparity within social economic classes in how justice is administered and the longer term generational implications especially to BIPOC, women and individuals with felony convictions. I came from privilege as a white make that had the economic resources to facilitate a defense within the system. I witnessed those not of my privilege suffer with longer sentences, harsher fines and worse. Then post incarceration I have witnessed how the laws punitively penalize those individuals for the rest of their life and cause further generational wealth depression for families.

    Over the decades I have worked with a number of political individuals on their campaigns and supported them via endorsements, contributions, or requests by them to vote for them and encouraged those in my inner circle to do so.

    I've had a good working relationship, despite my error in judgement thanks to forgiveness, with Governor Galvin Newsom, State Senator Bill Dodd and several regional San Francisco city and California state political leaders on a number of issues around the rights of LBGTQ individuals, BIPOC individuals and recommendations for policy change around HIV/AIDS policy, public health etc. while board president of a regional HIV related organization and in my roll at Goodwill with a re-entry program.

My hope is that our legislators will review this recommendation and act to level the playing field and help with job creation.

Occupational Licenses To Enhance Entrepreneurial Job Growth:

Out of Prison & Out of Work

San Francisco Bay Area

Author

&

Executive Coach

Chris Edwards

HISTORY OF OCCUPATIONAL LICENSING & THE IMPACT ON ENTREPRENEURSHIP & THE FORMERLY INCARCERATED
Chapter 1

This Book speaks from the point of view of criminal justice reform and there are significant references to the impact on post incarcerated individuals of the existing framework of Occupational Licensing and how reform will assist in job creation. However as a reader, please also review the proposed reforms from a standpoint of job creation and improving entrepreneurial opportunities within California and beyond.

For those outside of the state of California, this is a model position paper and applicable to what every state and the Federal Government should do, to reform Occupational Licensing and to enhance job creation opportunities across the nation.

From a criminal justice standpoint: most individuals that were formerly incarcerated want to work.

Many have acquired professional skills while incarcerated especially those in the Federal Prison Programs, that would add significant value to most professional organizations; if allowed to pursue the profession of choice, without governmental sanctioned barriers to entry.

Many individuals, while incarcerated receive college degrees through community college partnership programs. Others have in depth skills training on legal system filings through experience, others have gained skills in cosmetology, literacy teaching and other trades, of which they were proficient in learning while incarcerated. However, these skilled individuals are blocked from gaining fair pay employment due to governmental sanctions barriers in licensing them preventing them from entering those fields.

Historical perspective as related to jobs creation and protectionism within industries...

Interestingly state licensing for all but the most technical professions of medicine and law has expanded significantly in recent decades. Per the Goldwater Institute in a study by Morris Kleiner and Alan Kreuger, two of the foremost scholars on state licensing, have noted, *"in the early 1950s only about 5 percent of workers were covered by state licensing laws. Today, that number exceeds 20 percent of workers."*

State policymakers play a critical and longstanding role in occupational licensing policies, dating back to the late 19th century when the Supreme Court decision in Dent v. West Virginia established states' rights to regulate certain professions. Shortly after, states began developing their own systems of occupational regulation and licensing.

State policymakers play a central role in developing and shaping these systems by:

•	Establishing licensing requirements for specific occupations authorizing regulatory boards to license applicants and oversee compliance • Reviewing the merits of existing and proposed licensure requirements
•	Proposing strategies or guiding principles to improve the state's overall approach to regulating professions

"Of the 1,100 occupations that were licensed in at least one state in 2016, a small number (less than 60), were licensed in every state, illustrating the considerable differences in licensure requirements from state to state", according to the same source.

Every state licenses emergency medical technicians, bus and truck drivers, and cosmetologists, while three or fewer states license professions such as home entertainment installers, nursery workers, conveyor operators and florists.

Morris Kleiner, economics professor at University of Minnesota's Center for Human Resources and Labor Studies, asserted that, *"With growth of licensing laws has come a national patchwork of stealth regulation that has, among other things, restricted labor markets, innovation, and worker mobility."* Kleiner further asserted that, *"licensing resulted in 2.85 million fewer jobs nationally, with an annual cost to consumers of $203 billion."*

The Institute of Justice's 2012 License to Work Report ranked states based on the burdens imposed across 102 low and moderate income licensed occupations. The state comparisons revealed *"several inconsistencies across states: Many occupations are licensed in a small number of states, the same occupations have significantly different training requirements across states, and licensure requirements do not always align with public health or safety concerns."*

The inconsistency in licensing and the misnomer that the structure is in place to protect the public is what has created this anti-competitive layer of bureaucracy.

Researchers point out that *"cosmetologists require an average of 372 training days, significantly higher than emergency medical technicians, who need an average of 33 training days."* Researchers find little evidence that licensure improves the quality of services or protects consumers from harm.

In fact, evidence suggests that the most onerous licensure laws may lead to lower-quality services and increased public safety risks.

Licensing reduces the supply of service providers while simultaneously increasing the average operating costs for professionals.

The result of limited consumer choice and increased prices can be a provision of licensed services at a rate below true market equilibrium; in other words, consumers forego necessary services because prices are too high, or no one is available for hire.

This situation can pose a threat to public safety in certain occupations. For example, the inability to legally hire an electrician for repairs may lead to electrocution or fire. Similarly, licensing that limits the supply and increases the cost of veterinarians may prevent animal owners from vaccinating against contagious diseases like rabies.

According to a 2015 paper published by the Brookings Institution, *"economic studies have found little impact of occupational licensing on service quality in occupations that are not widely licensed; even in occupations that are widely licensed, studies have found few impacts of tougher requirements for licensing on health measures or quality outcomes."*

Further, a 2014 report from the U.S. Bureau of Labor Statistics on the safety of professionals in licensed industries concluded that *"the impact of occupational regulation on deaths and injuries is statistically insignificant."*

Economic research on professions that directly provide health and safety services has shown that licensing requirements may not achieve their intended goals.

A study on dental licensing found that dental office visits were reduced, and dental health outcomes were hindered because of *"licensure restrictions reducing employment."*

Similarly, a study of private security guard licensing found that lowering licensing burdens increased the supply of private security guards and was related to a significant drop in violent crime.

According to a 2015 brief published by the Council on Licensure, Enforcement and Regulation, *"civic leaders, elected officials, and courts have struggled to balance legitimate interests in protecting public health and safety with the preservation of free practice."*

Striking the right balance represents an opportunity for executive and legislative policymakers in California and beyond to achieve important public policy goals, including consumer protection, job creation, criminal justice reform, workforce mobility and economic growth.

Removing employment barriers for unique populations, such as immigrants with work authorization, military families, and people with criminal records, offers a powerful lever to achieve multiple policy goals. These include employment growth, reduced recidivism for employed ex-offenders, enhanced geographic mobility, and economic stability and opportunity for individuals and their families.

Barriers to Employment

The Goldwater Institute findings go further; *"Policymakers over the past few decades have rationalized that the growth of government licensing is necessary to protect the health and safety of the public at large. But the most robust explanation—which also explains the persistence of state licensing regimes—is that occupational licensing serves the purposes of keeping out new competitors."*

As such, it is favored mainly by incumbent businesses for that sole purpose. Note that any change as proposed will be a battle and the lobby dollars will come from business interests that are attempting to limit competition not for what is best for the state economy or job creation.

The Goldwater Institute findings continue; *"in truth, the health and safety justification rarely holds up under scrutiny. In cases where the policies have been studied, there is scant if any evidence that they enhanced the public's safety."*

From a criminal Justice Perspective: Structural barriers to securing employment, particularly within the period immediately following release are rampant for good paying jobs, when indeed they are most eager in their search, and the need for gainful employment is at its greatest.

For individuals, especially BIPOC individuals, women and members of the LBGTQ communities with a status of *"formerly incarcerated,"* their chance for fair paying employment are further hampered.

This perpetual labor market punishment creates a counterproductive system of release and homelessness in urban cores or significant poverty, hurting everyone involved: employers, the taxpayers, and certainly formerly incarcerated people looking to break the cycle of crime and become productive engaged citizens again. This additional burden hits rural communities disproportionately as well due to fewer job opportunities. Thus the rural states of the mid-west and the south and poorer inland communities of California carry these jobless opportunities burden in a more visible manner, then wealthier communities. However the homeless numbers in urban cores is increasing drastically of late as these individuals flee the rural areas in hopes of urban opportunities

Criminal justice research suggests that finding and maintaining a legitimate fair paying job can reduce a former prisoners' chances of reoffending. The higher the wage, the less likely it is that individuals will return to crime. The three years following release from prison is the window in which ex-prisoners are mostly likely to re-offend. Successful entry into the labor force has been shown to greatly increase the chances that a prisoner will not recidivate. Yet government imposed barriers to reintegration into the labor force, particularly occupational licensing requirements, can be among the most harmful barriers faced by ex-prisoners seeking to enter the workforce.

According to one estimate, there are currently over 12 million ex-felons in the United States, representing roughly 8% of the working-age population.(Uggen, Thompson, and Manza 2000).

It is estimated that roughly 2 Million ex-felons live within the state of California. Reintegration of released prisoners back into the workforce will be crucial to the eventual success of any criminal justice reform effort.

A first of its kind of study was commissioned by the Center for the Study of Economic Liberty to explore the relationship between three-year recidivism rates for new crimes and relate it to occupational licensing burdens by combining data from the Institute for Justice, the Pew Center on the States, and the National Employment Law Project. This study estimates that *"between 1997 and 2007 the states with the heaviest occupational licensing burdens saw an average increase in the three-year, new-crime recidivism rate of over 9%. Conversely, the states that had the lowest burdens and no such character provisions saw an average decline in that recidivism rate of nearly 2.5%."*

Some staggering statistics are to be found in a research document titled The Growth, Scope, and Spatial Distribution of People With Felony Records in the United States, 1948–2010 by Sarah K. S. Shannon1 & Christopher Uggen & Jason Schnittker & Melissa Thompson & Sara Wakefield & Michael Massoglia...

Barriers to Employment

"...15 % of the African American adult male population has been to prison; people with felony convictions account for 8 % of all adults and 33% of the African American adult male population."

The report further explains...
"People with any kind of criminal history experience wide-ranging penalties and disruptions in their lives, especially given the widespread availability of criminal background information (Lageson 2016; Uggen et al. 2014).

Nevertheless, people convicted of felonies face more substantial and frequently permanent consequences (Ewald and Uggen 2012; Travis 2005; Uggen and Stewart 2015).

A felony is a broad categorization, encompassing everything from marijuana possession to homicide. Historically, the term "felony" has been used to distinguish certain "high crimes" or "grave offenses" from less-serious, misdemeanor offenses."

People with felony records are set apart not only by the stigma and collateral consequences that come with a criminal conviction but also by the extreme concentration by sex, race, and socioeconomic status.

Current prison and community corrections populations are overwhelmingly male: 93 % of prisoners, 89 % of parolees, and 76 % of probationers (Carson and Golinelli 2013; Maruschakand Bonczar 2013).

Recent estimates have shown that 30 % of black males have been arrested by age 18 (vs. 22 % for white males) (Brame et al. 2014). This figure grows to 49 % by age 23, meaning that virtually one-half of all black men have been arrested at least once by the time they reach young adulthood (vs. approximately 38 % of white males) (Brame et al. 2014).

Western and Pettit have shown that incarceration has become a routine life event for low-skilled black men—more common than serving in the military or earning a college degree (Pettit and Western 2004; Western 2006).

The cumulative risk of imprisonment for black men ages 20–34 without a high school diploma stands at 68 % compared with21 % of black men with a high school diploma and 28 % for white men without a high school diploma (Pettit 2012).

According to a report by PrisonPolicy.org formerly incarcerated people are unemployed at a rate of over 27% — higher than the total U.S. unemployment rate during any historical period, including the Great Depression.

The American criminal justice system holds almost 2.3 million people in 1,719 state prisons, 109 federal prisons, 1,772 juvenile correctional facilities, 3,163 local jails, and 80 Indian Country jails as well as in military prisons, immigration detention facilities, civil commitment centers, state psychiatric hospitals, and prisons in the U.S. territories.

(The number of state facilities is from Census of State and Federal Correctional Facilities, 2005, the number of federal facilities is from the list of prison locations on the Bureau of Prisons website (as of March 14, 2019), the number of youth facilities is from the Juvenile Residential Facility Census Data book (2016), the number of jails from Census of Jails: Population Changes, 1999-2013, and the number of Indian Country jails from Jails in Indian Country, 2016)

Roughly 95% will eventually be released. Over 600,000 people make the difficult transition from prisons to the community each year according E. Ann Carson. 2018. Prisoners in 2016. Bureau of Justice Statistics.

Another startling statistic is every year, over 600,000 people enter prison gates, but people go to jail 10.6 million times each year. Via The Jail Reentry Round-table, Bureau of Justice Statistics statistician Allen Beck estimates that of the 12-12.6 million jail admissions in 2004-2005, 9 million were unique individuals.

Per PrisonPolicy.org more recently they analyzed the 2014 National Survey of Drug Use and Health, which includes questions about whether respondents have been booked into jail; from this source, they estimate that approximately 6 million unique individuals were arrested that year.

In a PrisonPolicy.org research document it was found that; *"among working-age individuals 25-44 the unemployment rate for formerly incarcerated people was 27.3%, compared with just 5.2%*

unemployment for their general public peers during the study period. That such a large percentage of prime working-age formerly incarcerated people are without jobs but wish to work suggests structural factors — like discrimination — play an important role in shaping job attainment."

While I personally have witnessed discriminatory practices in the hiring and interview process; they are also prevalent once individuals are employed in relation to promotions, pay equity and task assignments. However that is not the primary focus of this book it is worth noting and its impact on fair wage employment of those formerly incarcerated.

In a paper titled The Mark of a Criminal Records by Devah Pager, Northwestern University, he examined the effect of a criminal record in the labor market by sending out paired job testers (two white testers and two Black testers) where one tester in each pair was given a fictitious felony record. Pager's audit methodology allowed her to examine the independent effects of race and criminal records. Importantly, Black job testers without criminal records were less likely to receive callbacks from employers than white job testers with criminal records.

Although employer's express willingness to hire people with criminal records, evidence shows that having a record reduces employer callback rates by 50%. What employers say or believe they are doing contradicts what they actually doing in practice per another research report by Devah Pager and Lincoln Quillian titled, Walking the Talk? What Employers Say versus What They Do. American Sociological Review.

Based upon my experience with Goodwill Industries of the Greater East Bay, who's mission was to help place formerly incarcerated; I found that individuals want to work. A majority of the unemployment among this second chance population is a matter of public policy, and practice, biased hiring practices and not in the lack of aspirations for a better life.

Statistically, Black women who were formerly incarcerated are hit especially hard with severe levels of unemployment, whereas white men experience the lowest. Formerly incarcerated

Black women experience an unemployment rate 7 times that of the general population. Formerly incarcerated Black men experience unemployment 5 times that of the general population. When formerly incarcerated people do land jobs, they are often the most insecure and lowest-paying positions according to Gretchen Purser. 2012.

"Still Doin' Time:" Clamoring for Work in the Day Labor Industry. The Journal of Labor & Society.

According to an analysis of IRS data in a report by Adam Looney and Nicholas Turner. 2018 Work and opportunity before and after incarceration , ***"the majority of employed people recently released from prison receive an income that puts them well below the poverty line."***

This is even though many of these individuals have skills or experience in higher paying and professional occupations of which they are barred from due to government supported barriers to entry into those higher paying or more professional jobs.
So what have we learned in this chapter?

- Governmental sanctions via barriers in licensing harm job creation and economic growth
- In the early 1950s only about 5 percent of workers were covered by state licensing laws. Today, that number exceeds 20 percent of workers.
- Licensing does not necessarily create a safer workplace nor safeguards to the public good. • Rural communities are especially hard hit in job creation due to the over-reach of licensing boards
- 12 Million people are ex-felons clamoring for work, 2 Million within the state of California.
- The staggering numbers of Black individuals and especially Black Women that struggle the most in re-entry. We've seen the workplace, due to governmental sponsored barriers and ingrained bias, both racially and due to the stigma of incarceration, is not generally conducive to hiring formerly incarcerated individuals. • Th pathway out of poverty is stymied by these roadblocks which further harms socioeconomic development of these impacted individuals and thus their families and their communities.

Barriers to Employment

Good Intent Poor Results Chapter 2

Fact: Nearly 2 in 5 workers in the U.S. need State or Federal government permission just to do their jobs.

The intent of occupational licensure is to:
- Safeguard public health and safety.
- Protect consumers by guaranteeing minimum educational requirements and industry oversight.
- Support career development and pathways for licensed workers and enhanced professionalism for licensed workers.
- Step in when competitive market forces (e.g., litigation or reputation) fail to achieve desired outcomes.

However, unnecessary licensing requirements have been found to:
- Reduce employment in licensed occupations.
- Reduce geographic mobility.
- Reduce wages for unlicensed workers relative to their licensed counterparts.
- Reduce market competition and innovation.
- Increase the price of goods and services.
- Disproportionately burden low income and military veterans and families, people with a criminal history, immigrants with work authorization, and dislocated and unemployed workers. The Federal Trade Commission has asserted that unnecessary licensure regulations "erect significant barriers and impose costs that cause real harm to American workers, employers, consumers and our economy as a whole, with no measurable benefits to consumers or society."

Acting FTC Chairman Maureen Ohlhauser, recently asserted that *"occupational licensing disproportionately affects those seeking to move up the lower and middle rungs of the economic ladder, as well as military families and veterans, those* with criminal histories and those that have vocational skills but may not be college educated."

She noted that licensing requirements "can prevent individuals from using their vocational skills and entering new professions, as well as starting small businesses or creating new business models."

State policymakers play a critical and longstanding role in occupational licensing policies, dating back to the late 19th century when the Supreme Court decision in Dent v. West Virginia established states' rights to regulate certain professions. Shortly after, states began developing their own systems of occupational regulation and licensing. State policymakers play a central role in developing and shaping these systems by:

- Establishing licensing requirements for specific occupations
- Authorizing regulatory boards to license applicants and oversee compliance
- Reviewing the merits of existing and proposed licensure requirements
- Proposing strategies or guiding principles to improve the state's overall approach to regulating professions

According to a 2015 brief published by the Council on Licensure, Enforcement and Regulation, *"civic leaders, elected officials, and courts have struggled to balance legitimate interests in protecting public health and safety with the preservation of free practice."*

Striking the right balance represents an opportunity for state legislatures and those of the executive branches to achieve important public policy goals, including consumer protection, job creation, workforce mobility and economic growth. Removing employment barriers for unique populations, such as immigrants with work authorization, military families, and people with criminal records, offers a powerful lever to achieve multiple policy goals.

These include employment growth, poverty reduction in rural areas and urban inner cities, reduced recidivism for employed ex-offenders, enhanced geographic mobility, economic growth and

Barriers to Employment

increased tax base and economic stability and opportunity for individuals and their families.

One study in New York conducted by the National Institute of Justice showed ex-offenders were 50 percent less likely to receive callbacks or job offers. Employers are understandably reluctant to hire someone if they have a reason to think, right or wrong, that a job applicant could be untrustworthy or would somehow put customers at risk.

But what many may not know is that the law makes many occupations off-limits for people with a criminal record, even if an employer is willing to give them a chance.

Numerous licensing laws have morality clauses that (1) bar automatically and permanently ex-offenders from working without any individualized review or (2) require the ex-offender to prove a negative—that the ex-offender's past crimes will not cause him to harm customers in the future.

Such provisions ironically may decrease public safety. States with prohibitions and high burdens on entry have increasing criminal recidivism. Conversely, states that have no such bars and low burdens have seen declines in recidivism, according to Professor Stephen Slivinski's landmark study, Turning Shackles into Bootstraps.

Occupational licensing for individuals with criminal records face additional challenges finding and maintaining fair pay employment which is a critical aspect of reducing recidivism. Individuals with criminal records face many barriers to licensing including both those codified in federal and state law as well as implicit biases.

The National Inventory of Collateral Consequences of Conviction (the NICCC), catalogs over 15,000 provisions of law in both statute and regulatory codes that limit occupational licensing opportunities for individuals with criminal records.

According to Barriers to Work: People with Criminal Records Report from the National Counsel of Legislatures July 18, 2017: *"occupational licensing statutes in a number of states have blanket prohibitions on awarding of licenses to those with a criminal record. Some states' laws contain an automatic disqualification which prohibits a person with a felony conviction from obtaining an occupational license, regardless of whether the offense is directly related to the practice of the occupation or poses a substantive risk to public safety. In addition, licensing laws often contain "good-character" or "good moral character" provisions that grant licensing boards broad discretion to deny applications due to an applicant's criminal history, including convictions for minor offenses and sometimes arrests that never led to a conviction."*

The net result or negative side effect of these regulations or licensing requirements prevent people from starting a business and creating their own opportunity when no one else will hire them.

There is an effort the change the trend of the abuse or overreach of the rules from the prevailing war on crime during the most recent few legislative sessions across the US.
State legislatures across the country are moving more quickly and creatively to repair some of the damage done by the War on Crime, which left a third of the adult U.S. population with a criminal record. In the second quarter of 2019, 26 states have enacted an eye-popping total of 75 separate new laws aimed at addressing the disabling effects of a record – bringing the first-half total to 94 new laws enacted by 36 states. By way of comparison, in all of 2018 there were 61 new restoration laws enacted in 32 states and two territories, which was then a record, according to Collateral Consequences Resource Center
http://ccresourcecenter.org/

Most legislative attention was on facilitating access to record-clearing, although a significant number of new laws regulate consideration of criminal record in the occupational licensing process such as California SB2138 which was enacted into law in 2018 but does not take full effect until January 2021. California under Jerry Brown attempted to make changes under SB2138.

This was a good, first step.

Barriers to Employment

Assembly Bill 2138 was signed into law by Gov. Brown in September 2018. According to the bill, a licensing board cannot take away, or deny, a license on the basis of a criminal conviction if the following is true:

1. The conviction is seven years or older; and, (FLAW)
2. **The conviction is not substantially related to the job details the applicant will perform. (FLAW Open to broad interpretation)**

Please note, however, that these rules do not apply if a conviction is for a serious felony. That loophole is vague and allows for abuse and is a compromise that makes the intent of the law ineffective of its original charge.

This was a first step however, there are significant flaws in the law that need to be tweaked or addressed.

- The law still allows a ban on licenses when there was a conviction for "any act involving dishonesty, fraud, or deceit with the intent to substantially benefit himself or herself or another." If the applicant was convicted of a financial crime currently classified as a felony that is directly and adversely related to the fiduciary qualifications, functions, or duties of the business or profession for which the application is made" then a license may be denied. If the idea behind justice is rehabilitation and not punitive long term punishment, then once the sentence has been completed the individual should not be prohibited from entry or re-entry into a profession. However most criminal justice advocated would concur, that if after a second time, individuals, make a mistake and are convicted again of an offense, then they should have a lifetime ban.
- "A person shall not be denied a license solely on the basis that he or she has been convicted of a felony if he or she has obtained a certificate of rehabilitation", however this certificate s not issued in California or in many states for individuals that had cases in other state courts or in the Federal System.

- **7 Year Time frame Concern:** "...revise and recast those provisions to instead authorize a board to, among other things, deny, revoke, or suspend a license on the grounds that the applicant or licensee has been subject to formal discipline, as specified, or convicted of a crime only if the applicant or licensee has been convicted of a crime within the preceding 7 years from the date of application..." The 7 year time frame creates significant disadvantages to those re-entering the workforce or those attempting to move forward post incarceration with a fair-pay employment opportunity. The

timing of good job availability individuals post incarceration is critical to the reduction of recidivism.

We want convicted felons to overcome their criminal past. We want them to become productive members of the community. Yet we brand the with a "Scarlet F" that makes rehabilitation increasingly difficult.

Twenty-nine states allow occupational licensing boards to reject outright the application of someone with a criminal record Ex-convicts can't become school bus drivers, peace officers or employee at a children's treatment facility in most states. Even if the state licensing board must not automatically reject an ex-convict, there may be little to no restriction in state law to prohibit a licensing board from denying, at their discretion, a license based on the mere presence of a criminal record.

Eleven of the states can be called *"prohibition states,"* that is, they either automatically penalize ex-prisoners in the licensing processor have no other legal restrictions on the power of licensing board to base denial of a license on anything other than the presence of a criminal record, even for non-violent offenders or if the ex-prisoner's conviction; according to 2016 study from the National Employment Law Project (NELP).

Ex-convicts are usually unable to possess, obtain or maintain most professional licenses, certifications, or registrations. They're typically restricted from credentials for occupations in the Department of Public Health's jurisdiction or in real estate, the distribution of drugs or pharmaceuticals, pest control, embalming and insurance sales.

Barriers to Employment

In California, you are not going to get a license or credentialed if you are a doctor, athletic trainer, dentist, pawnbroker, psychologist, massage therapist, barber, nail salon operator, cosmetologist, contractor, veterinarian, social worker, physician's assistant and radiographer, physical therapist, and the ability to obtain a California alcoholic beverage license may also be affected by a prior felony conviction inhibiting job creation in the wine industry impacting many counties that have a significant employment base in that industry such as Napa, Sonoma, Lake, and those in the middle of the state.

Ex-convicts are not actually barred from practicing law in all states, but candidates are typically required to go through a waiting period, usually a minimum of five years, after being released from prison before restoring their civil rights. In Florida, this means candidates can attend law school but can't take the bar exam. Candidates in Texas wait five years before registering to take the bar – but the state notes that registering doesn't mean you will be allowed to practice.

At the federal level, a felony conviction may also result in the loss of a license, such as a customs broker's license; export license; license to export defense articles and services; merchant mariner's document, license, or certificate of registry; locomotive engineer's license, transportation worker identification credential (TWIC); and any other license, if the conviction is for a drug offense.

People convicted of a felony are ineligible to enlist in the Armed Forces unless they receive a waiver from the Secretary of Defense.

Ex-felons with tax consequences cannot even get a passport to leave the country or for employments with cruise lines or overseas with rare exception.

Recidivism Chapter 3

The revolving door of American's prison systems have proven very costly. The highest rate of "recidivism" (a relapse into crime and often, as a result, a return to incarceration) occurs within the first three years after release, nearly 68% of released prisoners recidivate during this time per Matthew R. Durose, Alexia D. Cooper, and Howard N. Snyder. "Recidivism of Prisoners Released in 30 States in 2005: Patterns from 2005 to 2010."

Estimates of how much can be saved in State and Federal budgets simply by helping these individuals avoid a return to prison reaches an average of at least $15.5 million annually. The total estimate of $635 million in budget savings resulting from a 10 percent decrease in the total recidivism rate comes from the Pew Center on the States, "State of Recidivism: The Revolving Door of America's Prisons," April 2011. This estimate is based on data from 41 states, hence the estimate quoted here of $15.5 million on average.

"This would be even higher for states that maintain a high per prisoner cost. Meanwhile, the costs to society, the economy, and to the former prisoners themselves, in the form of lost hours of labor, the social cost of higher crime rates, and the lost potential of the individual ex-prisoner, are immeasurable."

The greater the legal restrictions to working in a state, the higher the likelihood that an ex-prisoner will be turned away from entering the labor force and will return to crime hitting urban centers and the rural areas of a state hardest, thus increasing poverty and individual reliance upon government support programs.

A key component to Criminal Justice reform is to lower the rate of recidivism. Gainful employment is a key component post incarceration in making that happen.

Barriers to Employment

Policy Recommendations & Considerations Chapter 4

Occupational licensure requirements can have a range of effects on individuals with criminal records and policymakers across the country are considering ways to address those barriers. The policy options reviewed below focus specifically on those relevant to this population, but it is important to note that broader reforms can also affect individuals with criminal records. Information on broader tools and frameworks that can be used to help refine a state's regulatory approach are outlined in The State of Occupational Licensing: Research, State Policies and Trends.

It is worth noting that specific to this population as defined in statute, a states' policies should focus on the goals of seeking to encourage rehabilitation of criminal offenders while also protecting public safety and enhancing job creation within the state.

Modification of Morality Clauses

In order to create more transparency and fairness in the licensing process and, provide licensing entities more guidance in their treatment of criminal records, some states have chosen to remove vague and broad standards, such as "good moral character" and restrictions against "moral turpitude" offenses and provide more clarity on exclusionary convictions. This also allows potential applicants, with the specified offenses, to be more prudent in selecting occupations where those disqualifications are clear.

- As part of broader efforts on criminal justice reform, lawmakers in Kentucky disallowed licensing boards in the state from requiring that applicants possess vaguely defined *"good moral character."* Establish Pre-qualification Standards

Some states have mandated licensing entities to allow people with criminal records to petition the board for a "per-qualification" opinion. Pre-qualification allows an applicant to get a determination on eligibility before going through the licensing application process. In these cases, licensing boards are required to explicitly list disqualifying offenses and are able to notify applicants if their particular offense will disqualify them from licensure. This process helps ensure that people with criminal records, can devote their time and resources into occupations that will lead to gainful employment.

- In 2018, Arizona enacted legislation giving licensure applicants the authority to seek a predetermination from an agency as to whether the criminal record is a disqualifying offense for an occupational license.

Certification of Rehabilitation

Another policy option chosen by some states offers people with criminal records the opportunity to secure certificates of rehabilitation or certificates of employ-ability that would open the door to receiving occupational licenses.

Although the application of these certificates varies from state to state, they "may be used to provide a way for qualified people with criminal records to demonstrate rehabilitation or a commitment to rehabilitation, "and to relieve barriers to jobs and licenses. Certificates of rehabilitation may also be a viable option for states that have yet to adopt comprehensive record closure laws (expungement/sealing) since some are able to "directly limit the application of collateral consequences" while not removing information from a person's record or limiting public access.

- At least 12 states now make certificates of rehabilitation available through the court system and a few others through administrative agencies including California, Colorado, Illinois, North Carolina, Maryland, New Jersey, New York, Ohio, Rhode Island, Tennessee, Vermont, and Washington.
- **Note California offers this option only or those convicted of a state crime. There is no offer or consideration for those that were convicted in Federal Courts within the jurisdiction of California. The recommendation is that the existing law be modified to also include a Certification of Rehabilitation to those under-served individuals that are presently exempted from the benefits of the existing laws.**

Barriers to Employment

- Offering certificates of rehabilitation, which remove some of the employment restrictions imposed by occupational licensing statutes is an option

Another is a **"Certificate of Good Conduct"** which can be issued for anyone who goes either one year after release for a misdemeanor or two years after release from certain felonies without committing further crimes. These certificates also exempt employers from any "third-party liability" when they hire former offenders in some states.

Petitioning the court for any of these certificates can cost a lot of money. In California, which only Offers A Certificate of Rehabilitation for state offenses can cost from $1499 to $10,000 to gain once all legal fees and attorney fees are paid and again there is no such offering for those convicted of Federal Crimes within California and their pathway is further limited.

That kind of money is something many newly released and unemployed offenders don't have and further shows the inequity in the criminal justice system that negatively impacts those on the lower end of the economic spectrum in finding a way out.

Furthermore, people in this situation can't just wait a year or two for a certificate of good conduct when they need to support themselves and their families immediately upon release from prison.

Other states have enacted changes ...

Occupational licensing was the second most frequent area of law reform. Seven states, five in the South or Southwest, emerged from their legislative seasons this quarter having adopted proposals intended to give people significant new opportunities to join a regulated occupation or profession despite a criminal record, without unfair exclusions on vague "moral character" grounds:

- Arkansas went the farthest with the first revision of its licensing laws in 10 years, eliminating "good moral character" as a licensing criterion and prohibiting consideration of felony convictions after 5 crime-free years, sealed convictions, and pardoned convictions.

- Mississippi, Nevada and West Virginia for the first time imposed general procedural and substantive limits on their licensing boards.
- Texas further restricted its boards' discretionary authority to deny a license based on a conviction more than five years old, absolutely prohibited consideration of non-conviction records, and created a new "restricted license" in air-conditioning and electrical work aimed at people returning to the community from prison;
- Arizona made significant modifications to its licensing laws for the third year in a row, prohibiting consideration of felonies after 7 years, without regard to whether they have been set-aside.
- Alabama created a process allowing individuals to avoid mandatory bars on licensing via a court order of relief.
- New York eliminated statutory licensing barriers in many occupations.

Per the http://ccresourcecenter.org/2019/07/09/new-restoration-lawstake-center-stage-in-second-quarter-of-2019/#more-20013

As states consider occupational licensing policy options, data collection can also be an important piece of the governing language. Collecting applicant demographic data can help identify who is excluded from licensed work. Data collection also allows states to understand the effects of the licensing policy and be able to identify and address any gaps that may arise. However, a significant limitation to data collection is the inability to determine who is not applying for a license due to existing regulations or uncertainty of how standards are applied. Recognizing the barriers people with a criminal history face to entering the labor market, state policymakers across the country are actively addressing the challenges through legislation and executive orders.

Blanket bans, *"good moral character"* requirements and licensing fees can all be particularly difficult barriers for this population to overcome, which may ultimately be restricting a significant portion of workforce supply. Through policy options that include ensuring convictions are recent and relevant, the

Barriers to Employment

modification of statutory morality clauses and the implementation of prequalification standards or certificates of rehabilitation, policymakers can reduce unintended barriers to the labor market for individuals with criminal records.

Conclusion & Legislation Proposal or Revision Chapter 5

One of the primary concerns for people being released from prison is finding a job. But as our analysis illustrates, formerly incarcerated people are almost five times more likely than the general public to be unemployed, and many who are employed remain relegated to the most insecure jobs.

Note to Congressman Mike Thompson and Senators Kamala Harris and Senator Diane Feinstein; Congress has not attempted to deal with the problem of reintegration for more than a decade either by reducing federal collateral consequences or by restoring rights to people with federal convictions. It is time to act on behalf of those charged within the Federal System.

As more states and California explores reforming their criminal justice systems, much of the attention is likely to be paid to liberalizing sentencing laws, how and when to incarcerate someone and when probation or alternative means of punishment will suffice. Those reforms are extremely important and overdue. Yet those reforms, while valuable, don't address how best to reintegrate someone into the labor force once they have served their sentence.

Programs that have been aimed at helping formerly incarcerated increase their levels of educational achievement can be helpful, but these programs only overcome one aspect of re-integration into the labor force.

The government imposed hurdles for the formerly incarcerated will remain, regardless of education attainment or skill level, if the so-called "good character" provisions remain.

Moreover, while removing the "good character" provisions in occupational licensing laws will certainly help labor force reintegration, it will not deliver the biggest impact.

Liberalizing the occupational licensing burdens themselves and/or the skill level required and even the requirement that a license be required at all to work in a chosen occupation, will be the most likely to lead to widespread employment success for former prisoners and anyone with a criminal record.

A good source of information for consideration of the economic benefits to a state is a sunset process to licensing. A

Barriers to Employment

source study for a *"sunset process"* for occupational licensing regulations and insight on how such a process could work, see Stephen Slivinski, *"Bootstraps Tangled in Red Tape: How State Occupational Licensing Hinders Low-Income Entrepreneurship,"* Goldwater Institute Policy Report No. 272, February 23, 2015, available at:
http://www.goldwaterinstitute.org/en/work/topics/freeenterprise/entre preneurship/bootstraps-tangled-in-red-tape/

Entrepreneurship among low-income households and those of formerly incarcerated individuals has been shown in numerous studies to be an effective means of alleviating poverty and encouraging income mobility and reduce recidivism. Legislators and regulators would be well advised to advance a course of action that increases the potential for low-income entrepreneurship as one important tool in increasing prosperity and reducing poverty.

Broad-based reform of occupational licensing is a good idea from this perspective of job creation and state economic growth, not just from the perspective of its impact as a part of Criminal Justice Reform.

Incremental reforms can help achieve part of this goal. Requiring a review and potential sunset of most occupational licensing laws would put the burden of proof on those who advocate extending them and require them to prove the benefits of the regulations outweigh the costs, which should include the lower level of new business creation that results from these regulations.

Over time, it may become more obvious through such a review process that the health and safety regulations have outlived their usefulness, particularly in the face of new technologies, internet training and use of modern virtual educational systems. Sun setting entire classes of occupational licenses could provide an economic boom to California especially rural areas and urban inner cities and to any other state which implements these reforms. The side benefit to the criminal justice debate and might be the longer term goal.

There's no single remedy to fix the problem of ex-offender unemployment and the need for more job creation within states or the need to increase economic growth for entrepreneurs.
A simple blueprint modeled from the Institute on Justice includes the following actions…

- Repeal needless licenses—and refuse to adopt new ones. Examine current licenses: Is there empirical evidence of significant, widespread, and permanent harm in the field? Are there less restrictive alternatives to licensing? Repeal needless licenses and replace them, if necessary, with less restrictive regulations. Apply the same analysis when new licensing laws are proposed.
- Scale back anti-competitive licensing laws and policies Identify and eliminate "licensing creep"—anti-competitive licensing regulations, often imposed by licensing boards, which encroach on competing fields or outlaw innovative services. • Codify in statute the right to engage in a lawful occupation Give aspiring workers and entrepreneurs the chance to take unnecessary, anti-competitive licensing restrictions to court—and win.
- Implement meaningful sunrise and sunset reviews of licensing laws
    - Charge a non-partisan, independent agency with producing written reports evaluating the need or proposed and existing licenses.

Give it a mandate to use the inverted pyramid process to recommend less restrictive regulatory alternatives to licensing.
- Rein in anti-competitive behavior by licensing boards Establish an oversight body to actively supervise licensing boards. Give the oversight body a mandate to promote competition and favor less restrictive regulatory alternatives, curbing boards' tendency toward anticompetitive behavior and reducing the risk of federal antitrust liability.
- Strengthen the rights of people with a criminal record to gain meaningful employment

Barriers to Employment

Curtail license denials based on irrelevant or long-past criminal records.

Require case-by-case decisions on license applicants, demand substantial proof of risk of harm to deny a license, and allow applicants to seek a decision before investing in costly education, training, or testing

. • Improve interstate mobility first by eliminating licensing barriers

Before establishing reciprocity agreements or standardizing licensing requirements, ask whether there is substantial proof that licensing addresses a real problem. If not, tearing down licensing barriers is a better way to improve geographic mobility and expand economic opportunity.

- But part of the solution it is simple: let people work without asking the government's permission first.

This may not fix the ex-offender unemployment problem overnight. But government shouldn't be in the business of keeping people out of gainful and fair paying employment.

As citizens we are tasked with a responsibility to hold our government officials accountable to act in the best interest of the public for economic and personal liberty and security.

For our public legislator's nationwide and those within California mentioned in the introduction, the task before you is not an easy one but a noble one. You have the authority, there is public support for reform, the question before you is do you have the will-power against protectionism and lobbyist that use fear mongering to do what is right for more job creation?

On a more personal note, within California; Governor Gavin Newsom, State Senator Bill Dodd, Assembly Member Cecilia Aguiar-Curry & Congressman Mike Thompson you each can champion these changes and be examples to the nation.

What will be your legacy? Now the ball is in your court...

Proposed Model Legislation Occupational Licensing Review Act of 2019

SB2019 Senate Sponsor Bill Dodd
Assembly Sponsor Cecilia Aguiar-Curry

A bill for an act relating to occupational regulations; establishing the state policy for the regulation of occupations, specifying criteria for government regulation to increase opportunities, promote competition, encourage innovation, protect consumers; establishing canons of statutory interpretation; develop more entrepreneurship opportunities and job creation for at risk communities, eliminate protectionism policies inhibiting job creation, creating a process to review criminal history to reduce offenders' disqualifications from state recognition; comply with federal and state antitrust laws; and proposing coding for new law as _____, chapter _____.

BE IT ENACTED BY THE SENATE AND THE ASSEMBLY OF THE STATE OF CALIFORNIA:

100.01 Policy. For occupational regulations and their boards, it is the policy of the state that:

1. The right of an individual to pursue a lawful occupation is a fundamental right.

2. Where the state finds it is necessary to displace competition, it will use the least restrictive regulation to protect consumers from present, significant, and substantiated harms that threaten public health and safety.

3. Legislative leaders will assign the responsibility to review legislation and laws related to occupational regulations.

4. The governor will establish or further empower an office of antitrust with active supervision of occupational boards. The office is responsible for actively supervising the state's occupational boards to ensure no anti-trust violations consistent with the U.S. Supreme Court's ruling related to North Carolina State Board of Dental Examiners v. FTC

100.02 Definitions.

Subdivision 1. Scope. For the purposes of this chapter, the words defined in this section have the meaning given.

Barriers to Employment

Subd. 2. Government certification. "Government certification" means a voluntary, government-granted, and nontransferable recognition to an individual who meets personal qualifications related to a lawful occupation. Upon the government's initial and continuing approval, the individual may use "government certified" or "state certified" as a title. A non-certified individual also may perform the lawful occupation for compensation but may not use the title "government certified" or "state certified." In this chapter, the term "government certification" is not synonymous with "occupational license." It also is not intended to include credentials, such as those used for medical-board certification or held by a certified public accountant, that are prerequisites to working lawfully in an occupation. 2

Subd. 3. Government registration. "Government registration" means a requirement to give notice to the government that may include the individual's name and address, the individual's agent for service of process, the location of the activity to be performed, and a description of the service the individual provides. "Government registration" does not include personal qualifications and is not transferable but it may require a bond or insurance. Upon the government's receipt of notice, the individual may use "government registered" as a title. A non-registered individual may not perform the occupation for compensation or use "government registered" as a title. In this chapter, "government registration" is not intended to be synonymous with "occupational license." It also is not intended to include credentials, such as those held by a registered nurse, which are prerequisites to working lawfully in an occupation.

Subd. 4. Lawful occupation. "Lawful occupation" means a course of conduct, pursuit or profession that includes the sale of goods or services that are not themselves illegal to sell irrespective of whether the individual selling them is subject to an occupational regulation.

Subd. 5. Least restrictive regulation. "Least restrictive regulation" means, from least to most restrictive,

1. market competition,
2. third-party or consumer-created ratings and reviews,
3. private certification,
4. voluntary bonding or insurance,
5. specific private civil cause of action to remedy consumer harm,
6. deceptive trade practice act,
8 Registering with the secretary of state or other agency protects against fly-by-night providers.
9 Government certification is a voluntary signal that addresses the concern of asymmetrical information.
10 Specialty licenses allows for medical reimbursement without disputes over scope of practice.
7. mandatory disclosure of attributes of the specific good or service,2 8. regulation of the process of providing the specific good or service,3
9. regulation of the facility where the specific good or service is sold,4
10. inspection,5
11. bonding,6
12. insurance,7
13. government registration,8
14. government certification,9
15. specialty occupational license for medical reimbursement,10 and
16. occupational license.11

_____

_____ NOTE:
1 Deceptive trade practices acts are an effective means to protect consumers from fraud.
2 Mandatory disclosures may reduce misleading or confusing attributes. Disclosures that favor certain goods or services, such as a country-of-origin label, should not be used.
3 A housing/building code is an example of a regulation of a process; it may be more effective than enacting occupational licensing of tradesmen.

Barriers to Employment

4 A facility requirement may ensure that equipment, such as an eyewash station, is available to address accidents or emergencies.

5 Periodic inspections protect consumers from unsanitary facilities.

6 Requiring bonding protects against a provider's failure to fulfill contractual obligations.

7 Requiring insurance protects against a provider's damaging a consumer or third party.

8 Registering with the secretary of state or other agency protects against fly-by-night providers.

9 Government certification is a voluntary signal that addresses the concern of asymmetrical information.

10 Specialty licenses allows for medical reimbursement without disputes over scope of practice.

11 Only occupational licensing exposes board members to antitrust litigation, the 15 alternatives to licensing do not include that risk.

Subd. 6. Occupational license. "Occupational license" is a nontransferable authorization in law for an individual to perform exclusively a lawful occupation for compensation based on meeting personal qualifications established by the legislature. In an occupation for which a license is required, it is illegal for an individual who does not possess a valid occupational license to perform the occupation for compensation.

Subd. 7. Occupational regulation. "Occupational regulation" means a statute, rule, practice, policy, or other state law that allows an individual to use an occupational title or work in a lawful occupation. It includes government registration, government certification, and occupational license. It excludes a business license, facility license, building permit, or zoning and land use regulation except to the extent those state laws regulate an individual's personal qualifications to perform a lawful occupation.

Subd. 8. Personal qualifications. "Personal qualifications" are criteria related to an individual's personal background and characteristics. They may include one or more of the following: completion of an approved educational program, satisfactory performance on an examination, work experience, apprenticeship, other evidence of attainment of requisite knowledge and skills, passing a review of the individual's criminal record, and completion of continuing education.

Subd. 9. Private certification. "Private certification" is a voluntary program in which a private organization grants nontransferable recognition to an individual who meets personal qualifications and standards relevant to performing the occupation as determined by the private organization. The individual may use a designated title of "certified," as permitted by the private organization.

Subd. 10. Specialty occupational license for medical reimbursement. "Specialty occupational license for medical reimbursement" means a non-transferable authorization in law for an individual to qualify for payment or reimbursement from a government agency for the non-exclusive provision of new or niche medical services based on meeting personal qualifications established by the legislature. A private health insurance company or other private company may recognize this credential. Notwithstanding this specialty license, it is legal for a person regulated under another occupational regulation to provide similar services as defined in that statute for compensation and reimbursement. It is also legal for an individual who does not possess this specialty license to provide the identified medical services for compensation, but the non-licensed individual will not qualify for payment or reimbursement from a government agency.

100.03 Sunrise Review of Occupational Regulations.

Subdivision 1. Sunrise analysis of legislation involving occupational regulations. The Senate Committee on Business, Professions and Economic Development and the Assembly Committee on

Business and Professions in joint oversight will assign to their staff (hereafter 4 "staff") the responsibility to analyze proposals and legislation (1) to create new occupational regulations or (2) modify existing occupational regulations.

Barriers to Employment

Subd. 2. Sunrise reviews. (a) The staff is responsible for reviewing legislation to enact or modify an occupational regulation to ensure compliance with the policies in section 100.01.

(b) The staff will require proponents to submit evidence of present, significant, and substantiated harms to consumers in the state. The staff also may request information from state agencies that contract with individuals in regulated occupational and others knowledgeable of the occupation, labor-market economics, or other factors.

(c) The staff will determine if the proposed regulation meets the state's policy in section 100.01(2) of using the least restrictive regulation necessary to protect consumers from present, significant, and substantiated harms.

(d) The staff's analysis in (c) will employ a rebuttable presumption that consumers are sufficiently protected by market competition and private remedies, as listed in Section 100.02 subdivision 5 (1)-(4). The staff will give added consideration to the use of private certification programs that allow a provider to give consumers information about the provider's knowledge, skills and association with a private certification organization.

(e) The staff may rebut the presumption in (d) if it finds both credible empirical evidence of present, significant and substantiated harm, and that consumers do not have the information and means to protect themselves against such harm. If evidence of such unmanageable harm is found, the staff will recommend the least restrictive government regulation to address the harm, as listed in Section 100.02 subdivision 5 (5)-(16).

(f) The staff will use the following guidelines to form its recommendation in (e). If the harm arises from:

1. contractual disputes, including pricing disputes, staff may recommend enacting a specific civil cause of action in small-claims court or district court to remedy consumer harm. This cause of action may provide for reimbursement of the attorney's fees or court costs, if a consumer's claim is successful.

2. fraud, staff may recommend strengthening powers under the state's deceptive trade practices acts or requiring

disclosures that will reduce misleading attributes of the specific good or service;

3. general health and safety risks, staff may recommend enacting a regulation on the related process or requiring a facility license;

4. unclean facilities, staff may recommend requiring periodic facility inspections;

5. a provider's failure to complete a contract fully or to standards, staff may recommend requiring the provider to be bonded;

6. a lack of protection for a person who is not a party to a contract between providers and consumers, staff may recommend requiring the provider have insurance;

7. transactions with transient, out-of-state, or fly-by-night providers, staff may recommend requiring the provider register its business with the secretary of state;

8. a shortfall or imbalance in the consumer's knowledge about the good or service relative to the provider's knowledge (asymmetrical information), staff may recommend enacting government certification;

9. an inability to qualify providers of new or highly-specialized medical services for reimbursement by the state, staff may recommend enacting a specialty license for medical reimbursement;

10. a systematic information shortfall in which a reasonable consumer of the service is permanently unable to distinguish between the quality of providers and there is an absence of institutions that provide guidance to consumers, staff may recommend enacting an occupational license; and

11. the need to address multiple types of harm, staff may recommend a combination of regulations. This may include a government regulation combined with a private remedy including third-party or consumer-created ratings and reviews, or private certification.

(g) The staff's analysis of the need for regulation in (e) will include the effects of legislation on opportunities for workers, consumer choices and costs, general unemployment, market competition, governmental costs, and other effects.

Barriers to Employment

(h) The staff's analysis of the need for regulation in (e) also will compare the legislation to whether and how other states regulate the occupation, including the occupation's scope of practice that other states use and the personal qualifications other states require.

(i) The staff will report its findings and recommendations to the initial and subsequent committees that will hear the legislation. The report will include recommendations addressing:

1. the type of regulation, if any; 2. the requisite personal qualifications, if any; and

3. the scope of practice, if applicable.

(j) The staff also may comment on whether and how much responsibility the legislation delegates to a licensing board to promulgate administrative rules, particularly rules relating to establishing (a) the occupation's scope of practice or (b) the personal qualifications required to work in the occupation. The comment may make legislators aware of exposure to antitrust litigation that the legislation may cause because of excessive or ambiguous delegation of authority to licensing boards to engage in administrative rule making.

Subd. 3. Rule. The Assembly and the Senate will each adopt a rule requiring a committee considering legislation to enact or modify an occupational regulation to receive the staff's analysis and recommendations in subdivision 2 prior to voting on the legislation.

Subd. 4. Limitations. Nothing in section 100.03 shall be construed (1) to preempt federal regulation or (2) to require a private certification organization to grant or deny private certification to any individual.

100.04 Sunset Review of Occupational Licenses.

Subd. 1. Sunset analysis of existing occupational licenses.

(a)

Starting on January 1, 2020, the Senate Committee on Business,

Professions and Economic Development and the Assembly Committee on Business and Professions in joint oversight will assign to their staff (hereafter "staff") the responsibility to analyze existing occupational licenses.

(b) Each relevant standing committee of the legislature is responsible for reviewing annually approximately 20 percent of the current occupational licenses under the committee's jurisdiction. The committee chair will select the occupational licenses to be reviewed annually.

(c) Each relevant standing committee of the legislature will review all occupational licenses under the committee's jurisdiction within the subsequent five years and will repeat such review processes in each five-year period thereafter.

Subd. 2. Criteria. The staff will use the criteria in section 100.03 paragraphs 2(b)-(h) to analyze existing occupational licenses. 7 Subd. 3. Sunset reports. (a) Starting on January 1, 2021, the staff will report annually the findings of its reviews to the Speaker of the Assembly, the President of the Senate, Chairs of the relevant standing committees, the Governor, and the Attorney General. In its report, the staff will recommend the legislature enact new legislation that:

1. repeals the occupational licenses,
2. converts the occupational licenses to less restrictive regulations in section 100.02 subdivision 5,
3. instructs the relevant licensing board or agency to promulgate revised regulations reflecting the legislature's decision to use a less restrictive alternatives to occupational licenses;
4. changes the requisite personal qualifications of an occupational license;
5. redefines the scope of practice in an occupational license; or
6. reflects other recommendations to the legislature.

(b) The staff also may recommend that no new legislation is enacted.

Subd. 4. Limitations. Nothing in section 100.04 shall be construed (1) to preempt federal regulation, (2) to authorize the staff to review the means that a private certification organization uses to issue, deny or revoke a private certification to any

Barriers to Employment

individual, or (3) to require a private certification organization to grant or deny private certification to any individual.

100.05 Interpretation of Statutes and Rules. In construing any governmental regulation of occupations, including an occupational licensing statute, rule, policy or practice, the following canons of interpretation are to govern, unless the regulation is unambiguous: 1. Occupational regulations will be construed and applied to increase economic opportunities, promote competition, and encourage innovation;

2. Any ambiguities in occupational regulations will be construed in favor of workers and aspiring workers to work; and

3. The scope of practice in occupational regulations is to be construed narrowly to avoid burdening individuals with regulatory requirements that only have an attenuated relationship to the goods and services they provide.

4.

100.06-A Review of a Criminal Record.

Subdivision 1. Fundamental right. The right of an individual to pursue a lawful occupation is a fundamental right.

Subd. 2. Application. Notwithstanding any other law, a board, agency, department or other state agency (hereafter "board") will use only this chapter to deny, diminish, suspend, revoke, withhold or otherwise limit state recognition because of a criminal conviction.

Subd. 3. No automatic bar. A board will not automatically bar an individual from state recognition because of a criminal record but will provide individualized consideration.

Subd. 4. Information from a criminal record to be considered. A board may consider only a conviction of a non-excluded crime that is a felony or violent misdemeanor.

Subd. 5. Excluded information from a criminal record. A board will not consider:

1. non-conviction information from the criminal justice system including information related to a deferred adjudication, participation in a diversion program, or an arrest not followed by a conviction;

  2. a conviction for which no sentence of incarceration can be imposed;
  3. a conviction that has been sealed, dismissed, expunged or pardoned;
  4. a juvenile adjudication;
  5. a non-violent misdemeanor; or
  6. a conviction that occurred more than one year before the date of the board's consideration except for a conviction of:
   a. a felony crime of violence pursuant to statute section _____;
   b. a felony related to a criminal sexual act pursuant to statute section _____; or

  Subd. 6. **Rule of lenity.** (a) Any ambiguity in an occupational regulation relating to a board's use of an individual's criminal record will be resolved in favor of the individual.

  (b) The board will not use a vague term in its consideration and decision including:
  1. good moral character;
  2. moral turpitude; or
  3. character and fitness

  Subd. 7. **Included information.** The board will consider the individual's current circumstances including:
  1. the age of the individual when the individual committed the offense;
  2. the time since the offense;
  3. the completion of the criminal sentence;
  4. a certificate of rehabilitation or good conduct;
  5. completion of, or active participation in, rehabilitative drug or alcohol treatment;
  6. testimonials and recommendations including a progress report from the individual's probation or parole officer;
  7. other evidence of rehabilitation;
  8. education and training;
  9. employment history;
  10. employment aspirations;
  11. the individual's current family responsibilities; and

Barriers to Employment

    12.   other information that the individual submitted to the board.

    Subd. 8. Hearing. The board will hold a public hearing, should the individual request one, pursuant to section _____ of the state's administrative procedure act.

    Subd. 9. Totality of the circumstances test. (a) The board may deny, diminish, suspend, revoke, withhold or otherwise limit state recognition only if the board determines:

    1.   the state has an important interest in the regulation of a lawful occupation that is directly, substantially and adversely impaired by the individual's non-excluded criminal record as mitigated by the individual's current circumstances in subdivision 7, and

    2.   the state's interest outweighs the individual's fundamental right to pursue a lawful occupation.

    (b) The board has the burden of making its decision by clear and convincing evidence.

    Subd. 10. Appeal. The individual may appeal the board's decision as provided for in section _____ of the state's administrative procedure act.

    100.06-B Petition for Board Determination Prior to Obtaining Personal Qualifications.

    Subd. 1. Petition. An individual with a criminal record may petition a board at any time, including before obtaining any required personal qualifications, for a decision whether the individual's criminal record will disqualify the individual from obtaining state recognition.

    Subd. 2. Content. The individual will include in the petition the individual's criminal record or authorize the board to obtain the individual's criminal record.

    Subd. 3. Determination. The board will make its decision using the criteria and process in section 100.03.

    Subd. 4. Decision. The board will issue its decision no later than 60 days after the board receives the petition or no later than 90 days after the board receives the petition if a hearing is held.

The decision will be in writing and include the criminal record, findings of fact and conclusions of law.

Subd. 5. Binding effect. A decision concluding that state recognition should be granted or granted under certain conditions is binding on the board in any later ruling on state recognition of the petitioner unless there is a relevant, material and adverse change in the petitioner's criminal record.

Subd. 6. Alternative advisory decision. If the board decides that state recognition should not be granted, the board may advise the petitioners of actions the petitioner may take to remedy the disqualification.

Subd. 7. Reapplication. The petitioner may submit a revised petition reflecting completion of the remedial actions before a deadline the board sets in its alternative adviser decision.

Subd. 8. Appeal. The petitioner may appeal the board's decision as provided for in section _____ of the state's administrative procedure act.

Subd. 9. Reapply. The petitioner may submit a new petition to the board not before one year following a final judgment on the initial petition or upon obtaining the required personal qualifications, whichever is earlier.

Subd. 10. Cost. The board may charge a fee to the petitioner to recoup its costs not to exceed $100 for each petition.

100.06-C Reporting. (a) The Senate Committee on Business, Professions and Economic Development and the Assembly Committee on Business and Professions direct the appropriate state department to establish an annual reporting requirement of the:

1. number of times that each board acted to deny, diminish, suspend, revoke, withhold or otherwise limit state recognition from a licensed individual because of a criminal conviction;

2. offenses for which each board acted in sub paragraph 1;

3. number of applicants petitioning each board under section 100.04,

Barriers to Employment

    4.   numbers of each board's approvals and denials under section 100.04,

    5.   offenses for which each board approved or denied petitions under section 100.04, and

    6.   other data the Department determines.

(b) The Department will compile and and publish annually a report on a search-able public website.

100.06-D Limitation. Nothing in this chapter shall be construed to require a private certification organization to grant or deny private certification to any individual.

100.07 Office of Antitrust and Active Supervision of Occupational Boards.

Subdivision 1. Antitrust law. By establishing and executing the policies in section 100.01, the state intends to ensure that occupational boards and board members will avoid liability under federal antitrust laws.

Subd. 2. Active Supervision. To help execute the policies, the governor will establish the California Office of Antitrust and Active Supervision of Occupational Boards reporting to the Governor with annual reports to the joint Senate Committee on Business, Professions and Economic Development and the Assembly Committee on Business and Professions

Subd. 3. Responsibility. The office is responsible for the active supervision of the state's occupational boards to ensure compliance with section 100.01, the applicable licensing statutes, and federal and state antitrust laws. Active supervision requires the office to play a substantial role in the development of boards' rules and policies to ensure they (a) benefit predominantly consumers and (b) do not benefit unreasonably or serve merely private interests of providers who the boards regulate.

Subd. 4. Approval. The office will exercise control over boards' processes and substantive actions to ensure they are consistent with section 100.01, the applicable licensing statutes, and federal and state antitrust laws. The office must review, and approve or reject any proposed board rule, policy, enforcement, or other regulatory action prior to it being adopted or implemented. The office's approval must be explicit; silence or failure to act will not be deemed approval.

Subd. 5. Personnel. The office personnel must be independent of boards. A government or private attorney who provides general counsel to a board will not also serve in the office.

Subd. 6. Cost Allocation. The office may assess its costs on each board for the services of active supervision. Each board may recoup the assessment by increasing the fees paid by license holders.

100.08 Effective date. This chapter is effective on January 1, 2020.

NOTE A model of Federal Legislation or model that this was based upon but is located at the Institute of Justice at: https://ij.org/wp-content/uploads/2019/03/03-20-2019-OccupationalLicensing-Review-Act-1.pdf

For a professional analysis or more information
Contact information:
Lee McGrath
Meagan Forbes Counsel Legislative Counsel
lmcgrath@ij.org mforbes@ij.org
Institute for Justice
520 Nicollet Mall-Suite 550
Minneapolis MN 55402-2626

Barriers to Employment

Information Sources/BIBLIOGRAPHY

- Goldwater Institute in a study by Morris Kleiner and Alan Kreuge
- The Institute of Justice's 2012 License to Work Report
- 2015 Brookings Institution Report on

  Licensing 2014 Report from the U.S.

  Bureau of Labor Statistics

- Gretchen Purser. 2012. The Journal of Labor & Society.
- Center for the Study of Economic Liberty
- 2015 brief published by the Council on Licensure, Enforcement and
- Regulation
- The Growth, Scope, and Spatial Distribution of People With Felony
- Records in the United States, 1948–2010 by Sarah K. S. Shannon1
- & Christopher Uggen & Jason Schnittker & Melissa Thompson &
- Sara Wakefield & Michael Massoglia
- Census of State and Federal Correctional Facilities, 2005
- E. Ann Carson. 2018. Prisoners in 2016. Bureau of Justice Statistics.
- Per PrisonPolicy.org & the 2014 National Survey of Drug Use and
- Health
- The Mark of a Criminal Records by Devah Pager, Northwestern University
- Devah Pager and Lincoln Quillian titled, <u>Walking the Talk? What Employers Say versus What They Do.</u> American Sociological Review.

- According to an analysis of IRS data in a report by Adam Looney and Nicholas Turner. 2018 Work and opportunity before and after incarceration ,
- Reports by Devah Pager and Lincoln Quillian titled, Walking the Talk? What Employers Say versus What They Do. American Sociological Review.
- Barriers to Work: People with Criminal Records Report from the National Counsel of Legislatures July 18,2017
- Gretchen Purser. 2012. "Still Doin' Time:" Clamoring for Work in the Day Labor Industry. The Journal of Labor & Society.
- The Federal Trade Commission
- Collateral Consequences Resource Center http://ccresourcecenter.org/
- 2015 brief published by the Council on Licensure, Enforcement and
- Regulation,
- Center for the Study of Economic Liberty at Arizona State University Professor Stephen Slivinski's landmark study Turning Shackles into Bootstraps.
- Matthew R. Durose, Alexia D. Cooper, and Howard N. Snyder. "Recidivism of Prisoners Released in 30 States in 2005: Patterns from 2005 to 2010." April 22, 2014, Bureau of Justice Statistics, NCJ 244205, available at:
- HTTP://www.bjs.gov/index.cfm?ty=pbdetail&iid=4986
- Pew Center on the States, "State of Recidivism: The Revolving Door of America's Prisons," April 2011, available at: http://www.pewtrusts.org/en/research-andanalysis/reports/0001/01/01/state-of-recidivism.
- Matthew R. Durose, Alexia D. Cooper, and Howard N. Snyder. "Recidivism of Prisoners Released in 30 States in 2005: Patterns from 2005 to 2010.
- Pew Center on the States, "State of Recidivism: The Revolving Door of America's Prisons," April 2011.

- Michelle Natividad Rodriguez and Beth Avery, "Unlicensed and Untapped: Removing Barriers to

Barriers to Employment

Occupational Licenses for People with Records," National Employment Law Project, April 2016, available at http://www.nelp.org/publication/unlicensed-untappedremoving-barriers-stateoccupational-
- licenses/
- 2015 brief published by the Council on Licensure, Enforcement and Regulation.
- The Institute of Justice's 2012 License to Work Report

About The Author

Chris Edwards was born in Shawneetown, Illinois and spent his formative years around Nashville, Tennessee. Chris Edwards has lived for 25 years in California and most recently New Mexico. He is a recognized proponent of the cultural arts, a strong business leader and a political activist for equality in human rights, the rights of POC and LBGTQ+ causes. Chris has traveled to 46 countries and enjoys the diversity of cultures. Chris Edwards has led divisions of large public companies, assisted with the growth and support of social enterprises, and served on boards of several non-profits.

Chris Edwards, is recognized as a mentor, in teaching those around him the skills of positive self-esteem. Chris's releases have ranked in the Amazon top 100 in "Self Esteem Self Help" and in "Self Help Short Reads" and his collaborative effort with co-author Rene Sepulveda; Coach Robert Sepulveda the early years book 1 launched as a #1 New Release for several weeks in the Football Coaching Category.

Chris Edwards releases include 90 Days to a Glass Half Full Lifestyle and 2 Hours Unplugged: Unplug & Reconnect and is a continuation of that series. 2 Hours Unplugged: Unplug & Reconnect launched as a #1 New Release on Amazon in the "Information Theory" Category containing books on technology and their impact to quality of life.

Chris has partnered with RENE SEPULVEDA MPH, CPT on a series of fitness books and other projects. Their more recent collaboration is a series on Coach Robert and Marilyn Sepulveda. This book series, beginning with book 1 of a 3 part series, is an Alamogordo Tiger Tale of the Historical Crossroads of Football, Track & Field and Cross Country, In Building New Mexico Pride. The book series begins with the Alamogordo, New Mexico athletic program in 1916 and progresses through today with a national scope and focus on interscholastic sports.

The book is a comprehensive history that tells the stories of the many personalities from 1916 to 1996 that influenced New Mexico interscholastic sports in Track and Field, Cross Country, High School Football and beyond. Coach Bob Sepulveda had the

Barriers to Employment

longest consecutive State Track & Field Winning streak in the 90s of any New Mexico Coach. The book highlights the records and the stories of hundreds of athletes.

The book series takes on the tough issues of the launch of national high school interscholastic sports standards, integration in the 50's and 60's, Title IX implementation and girls interscholastic championships, the politics around high school football and more. The book series contains the records of 100s of high school athletes, rich in dialog and interviews with athletes, coaches, and community members. It tracks the successes and failures of some great athletes & coaches.

The central characters in the book series are Coach Bob and Marilyn Sepulveda paired with a variety of characters that played a role in the program success of the Alamogordo, New Mexico Track and Field, Cross Country & Football programs.

While the series storyline is focused on a small town in New Mexico; it is national in scope; as many associated coaches and athletes had a national or international influence in athletics, politics, the Olympics and world events. The series common theme is all were touched by the Alamogordo Track & Field, Cross Country or Football programs, Coach Bob Sepulveda and his associated legacy.

For opportunities to learn more about
Chris Edwards, mentoring or fitness sessions and collaborative efforts visit https://2ndlifemedia.com

pg. 52 Author Chris Edwards San Francisco Bay Area

Learn more 2nd Life Media
https://2ndlifemedia.com

www.ingramcontent.com/pod-product-compliance
Lightning Source LLC
Chambersburg PA
CBHW030010190526
45157CB00015B/2225